What Surrounds You

What Surrounds You

Poems by

Roxanne Doty

Cover design by Shay Culligan
Cover image is an illustration by Paul Nash (1889–1946) from
Thomas Browne's *Urne-Buriall and The Garden of Cyrus* (1932),
courtesy of Birmingham Museums Trust on Unsplash
Author photo by Don Laurence Photography

ISBN: 979-8-90146-729-9
Library of Congress Control Number: 2026936261

Kelsay Books
502 South 1040 East, A-119
American Fork, Utah 84003
Kelsaybooks.com

Acknowledgments

My sincere thanks to the members of my writing groups whose feedback and support is invaluable, and to the writers in the greater Phoenix area and beyond who listened to and read my work and provided so much support and encouragement. Much appreciation to Changing Hands Bookstore's First Friday Poetry and Esso Coffeehouse for providing such wonderful venues for Phoenix area poets to share work that always inspires.

Gratitude to the following publications, where versions of these poems previously appeared:

Amethyst Review: "Damavand, 1977"
Anti-Heroin Chic: "La Loba"
Blue Guitar: "My Grandmother's Palimpsest," "The Ghosts of Old Phoenix," "QT QuickTanning Lotion by Coppertone," "My mesquite tree," "The First Three Days," "To Carry On"
Cagibi: "Standing on the Long Island Expressway Overpass in Queens, New York"
Cloudbank: "Peralta"
Gyroscope Review: "Reunion"
I-70 Review: "Quick Wash"
International Times: "American Night," "The World We've Left Our Children"
Little Somethings Press: "Lipstick 205"
New Verse News: "Interview with the Dean"
The Orchards Poetry Journal: "Blizzard," "Blood Sisters"
Passengers Journal: "Furnishings," "Girls, 1969"
San Pedro River Review: "Used Books,"
Sequestrum: "Fountain Pen," "Midnight at a truck stop in Terre Haute, Indiana," "Superman"

Third Wednesday: "There's a police car in front of the house and Dad is standing in a puddle of rain water," "Omar"
Unstrung: "The phoenix bird," "Where Did You Sleep Last Night, Lavigne?"
Verse-Virtual: "The Saguaros of Pass Mountain"

Contents

I

I

Blizzard

The snow falls for days,
buries dead winter grass
and bare spots of hard dirt,
covers us in a soft blanket
of stillness, erases boundaries
between houses, one yard
and the next, streets
and sidewalks, earth and sky,
you and me.

Wind blows it into great drifts.
No school buses, no work,
everything cancelled,
our world a clean page.
You make coffee in a stained pot.
The smell spreads through the house.
You will not reach for a drink.

I walk through mounds of white
above my knees,
roll the new snow in my hands
until it holds together.
Fragile as glass, flakes
like tiny mirrors. I see our other selves,
the ones we can never be.
The heat of my gloved hand
melts the mirror crystals.
They drip to the ground and evaporate.

One Inch Equals Fifteen Miles

The first thing I learned to read
was a map.
My father held it in his hands
like a prayer
spread it across the dash
wiped away the ashes
fallen from his Camel cigarette,
smoothed the creases
and showed me the state of Missouri.

This is where we are.
His nicotine-stained finger
pointed to St. Louis.
We were in the parking lot
of an old motor lodge.
Two weeks we'd been there.
He couldn't make up his mind
where to go next
where jobs might be.

He pulled out another map
laid it next to the first
and traced a line of deep blue
from St. Louis until his finger
touched Nashville.
This is where we came from.

One inch equals fifteen miles, he said.
I asked him where we were going.
He shrugged.

Kansas City was sixteen inches away,
Columbia, eight inches.
He said he didn't know yet,
but we could find our way
with those maps.

Cascade

Scent of chlorine and summer
aquamarine water ripples in the sun.
I splash into the deep end
a public pool called Cascade
plunge with no fear
my head bobs from the water
your arms lift me high
above the other swimmers.
You smile, dark hair dripping
shimmering droplets down your face
over fine lines around your eyes
teeth white like pearls
on the necklace Grandma wears to church
the sweet smell of pipe tobacco
on your breath, my entire world
this moment of absolute purity, security
a brief space of time before sadness
confusion, a moment which survives
only in vivid and flawed memory.

The House on Charlotte Street

A front porch swing
slanted cellar door
reading nook, bay window
lilac bushes in summer
crystal snow in winter
our red Mercury station wagon
in the driveway after burning distance
heat shimmer dancing in sunlight
St. Christopher medal dangling
destination just a rumor
until that single moment
of arrival in the city of union jobs
fresh starts, the ramshackle house
looked like home, a stray cat
lounging on the swing
watching as if it understood
how easily we could break

Union Station

It's always early morning at Union Station
Pershing Road, Kansas City
Beaux-Arts architecture, fountains in front
three arched entries to the Grand Plaza
chandeliers suspend from coffered ceiling
marble floors, the long North Hall
waiting room with wood benches
like church pews, train whistles
clanging brakes, arrivals and departures
your Juicy Fruit chewing gum breath
sea shell hair combs, rosary beads
in your purse, goodbyes and distance
absences yet to come, learning
that neither of us would live forever.

My Grandmother's Palimpsest

The radio played Nat King Cole
every day that summer in Nashville.
My grandmother said his voice was liquid
and I thought of root beer soda
from the candy store down the street,
soothing and perfect like a soft hand
on your shoulder. I loved *Ramblin' Rose,*
wanted to be like her, wild and windblown.
I was ten.

That summer my grandmother learned
her favorite singer was black.
Oh mother, my mom said, annoyed
and impatient. *You never saw a photo?*
And what difference does it make?
We had his albums but my grandmother
only had Nat King Cole's voice on her radio.
She shook her head and stopped listening
denied she ever treasured him.

My grandmother didn't look the same
after that. I still loved her.
Loved her Juicy Fruit chewing gum
and ivory hair clip, the bingo games
on Friday nights. But, I blamed her
for the *whites only* sign at the laundry mat,
and the white ladies at Christ the King
who wiped the pews after black
church-goers sit in them.

When a black family moved next door,
I was only allowed to play
with my new friend, Shirley
who was ten like me, outside.
I can't have her in my house,
my grandmother said.

We moved to New York in the fall
and my grandmother's words faded
but they were never erased. Effaced
and written over, they echoed
through my childhood, bore traces
of the old words, ugliness ebbing
and rising again and again tainting
our world, the world we leave
our children.

That summer in Nashville comes back
with a sad fury, but Nat King Cole's words
remain unspoiled, beautiful to hold onto.
Wild and windblown. Who will love you
with a love true? I stopped thinking
of my grandmother when I heard them,
just that man and his liquid voice.

Nashville Days, 1963

On the way to Sunday night bingo, a siren
screams as an ambulance races
through the intersection, the light
red but that doesn't matter
Grandma Muh makes a sign of the cross
and whispers a short prayer

one I learned at St. James, the prayer
to the Virgin Mary, the night quiet except for the siren
whose sound fades as we cross
the street to bingo, these Nashville days race
like no other time in my short life, they matter
the way things about life come to light

bingo is in a huge room with fluorescent light
I want to win money for mom but there isn't a prayer
she just smiles, says it doesn't matter
kids can't win and when someone gets bingo, a siren
sounds like that ambulance or a whistle to start a race
the winner's card filled in numbers diagonal, down or across

the year fills with sad news I come across
ugly truths under glaring light
some of my childhood begins to race
away from me and I develop doubts about prayer
like the ones Muh whispers at the sound of a siren
as if the lives of others really matter

I learn new things about my 12-year-old self that matter
sufferings in the world, humans bearing a cross
days full of emergencies louder than that siren

so many names and words come to light
John F. Kennedy, Birmingham, Bull Connor—beyond the help of prayer
the world falls down with violence and hate around a thing called *race*

A new thing I to try to understand racing
through my young mind, why does it matter
is there a prayer
to erase the ugliness with a powerful cross
and gentle, benevolent light
bury it with the blare of a siren

Repossession

A toss of stars
across a November night sky
snow-covered yard, red Mercury
station wagon in the drive.

The next morning a bare space
of cold dirt and dead grass glares
like rage, swallows your dreams
spits them out, the red Mercury gone.

You pace the kitchen, work shoes
squeak against linoleum. Authorities
tell you the bank owns the car now.
Your tools in the trunk paid in full.
What about them? The officer shrugs.
And the St. Christopher medal
that hung from the rearview, protected us
on so many highways?

When they leave, you sit at the table,
smoke a pipe. *They own everything,*
you say and I wonder about my roller skates.
Tobacco smoke swirls around you.

Two Dresses

One deep red, jersey fabric, tailored
straight skirt, big loops
for a black patent leather belt.
I called it your Kennedy dress
because you wore it to see John Kennedy
campaign, Dad in a good mood.
The other dress is black rayon
silk waistband, low-cut neckline.

I stand before them in your closet
long slashes down the front
how many I wonder and count
one, two, more than two, too many
to fix, sew up, make whole again
and I briefly think a burglar did this
after he overturned the dining room table
chairs strewn about the room
like a cyclone ripped through the house.
You stand stoic and silent
unlit cigarette in your hand, say calmly
Annie, get me some matches
off my dresser and now I want to grab
the matches and close the closet door
pretend I didn't see the dresses
hoping they will disappear
but instead I understand.

I try to imagine how it all unfolded
try to recall where we were
as he flung the table over, slashed the dresses
maybe it was at the exact moment
I was laughing with the nice woman
who cut my hair and did my first perm
feeling very sophisticated for eight years old
or maybe we were waiting for the 4pm bus
from downtown.

Dad doesn't come home for a week.
Part of me wants him to never come home
but he shows up Sunday morning
all smiles, handsome and relaxed
sets a big shopping bag on the table
upright again thanks to my brother.
How's my girl? He asks
ruffles my short curly hair
looks at me with a funny face
and makes me laugh.
Fine, I say.

Superman

He likes to stop at a bar
on the lower east side of Manhattan
before we head home.
I'll be right back, he says
as he parks the car.
Keep the doors locked.
And he disappears
around the corner.
I imagine Clark Kent
changing into Superman,
off to rescue someone
in this place we call *the city.*

I check the locks, a light drizzle
taps steady on the roof
windows fog, the newspaper stand
closes and the street is silent.
I imagine Lois Lane
sitting next to my father in the bar
looking at him as if she suspects
he might not be who he appears to be.

He returns to the car. *Ready?*
He asks as if he's been waiting
for me in the cold damp.

He places his pipe in the ashtray
turns around and flashes a quick smile
the grainy smell of beer on his breath,
then a blur of headlights, taillights
streetlights. Superman flies
over us as we approach the Midtown tunnel.

Stateline Road

Stateline Road was the happiest
in our broken family, Kansas on our side,
Missouri on the other.
Amusement park on Sundays,
our red Mercury station wagon,
we in the back seat facing the street,
could see where we'd just been.
Dad built me a rope swing,
sawed holes in a piece of wood
ran a rope through them
and hung it from a tree. Told me
if I pumped hard enough.
my feet could touch the sky.
It was the happiest time
until my brother told me about the soup
thrown all over the kitchen floor
the fights, the cops at the door.

Burnt Coffee

Coffee burns on a blazing stove
switched on in the blur
of a lonely midnight attempt
at sobriety, the kettle's whistle rises
to a relentless scream, warning
of impending explosion, coffee grounds
will shoot from the small opening
brown liquid splatter over the edges
of our lives, onto the walls
and still the burning will continue
the smell seeping under my bedroom
door as I listen to your unsure footsteps
slurred curses as the stainless-steel kettle
slams against a cold, hard floor.

I venture from the safety of my room
into this war zone of spewing coffee
ashtray overflowing and you
emerge from your numb anger
a look of surprise, shame and something
resembling vague and distant happiness
appears on your almost-still-handsome face
as you muster all the lingering control
left in your drunken soul and say
hello little girl and a tired peace
settles over us.

Furnishings

My father was a rebel, a nomad who routinely packed up our meager possessions and headed down the highway chasing undefined, illusive dreams that moved too fast for him to capture and he should have known better than to let the American ideal snare him and his restless soul by taking out a mortgage on a small three-bedroom bungalow in a suburban development of identical three-bedroom bungalows and furnishing it with old furniture from my renegade grandmother's apartment on West 74th from which she had been evicted because of urban renewal, but refused to go until they put her belongings on the sad street in front of the six-story, pre-war building slated for demolition. He purchased two table lamps from E.J. Korvettes discount department store at Walt Whitman Mall wrapped in cellophane to be removed when brought home but he insisted it be left on as if his commitment to a settled life was embodied in those two lamps that had to be protected and preserved though the cellophane dried out, cracked, collected dust and became a source of argument along with all the other sources of argument until mom moved out, taking my sister with her while I stayed mostly because of the loneliness in his eyes and the tragedy of him burying his longing to wander. Sometimes when he was at work at Sam's deli having quit the plumbers' union because he didn't like following other people's rules and had also left the janitor's job at Little Plains Elementary because he didn't like cleaning up other people's shit, I'd sit in the living room and watch sun beams shine through the window, cut through the crumbling cellophane still on the lamps, rays of resplendent dust gliding on shafts of light and though I knew I was really looking at fine particles of soil, dirt, dead skin cells and fecal matter of dust mites built up over the years as deterioration surrounded us, I still marveled at the radiance and remembered my father's face from his itinerant days when he sat in the car at some motel, studying a map, a smile on his handsome face.

Work

The way it stained your hands
leached into crevices of skin
settled under broken fingernails
the industrial smell of Borax
on the kitchen counter your eyes
far away.

But sometimes snow, crystal manna
from the sky and the way you stood
in front of your old Mercury
scraper in hand
and how you paused to gaze
at the shimmer.

Cold vapor with each exhale
you smiled as if all the white
had delivered us
a chance.

There's a police car in front of the house and Dad is standing in a puddle of rain water

in the gutter next to where he parked and the officer has exited his patrol car and they are chatting under the street lights that shines on them like rays from an impossible heaven as dad reaches into his pocket and pulls out his wallet and driver's license which he passes to the cop, both of them seeming oblivious to that pool of water, more a lake than a puddle, that always forms after a heavy rain like the one we had the day before, a cold winter downpour, the air still damp and chilled and I watch from my bedroom window, open it enough to hear what they say, wondering how many Budweisers he had at *Sam's Bar* or the *Chat-A-While* or *The 19th Hole* before he headed home and if the cop will give him a ticket or arrest him or take away his license like before when he had to ride his bike everywhere and the old Mercury sat sadly in the drive way for the longest time but dad is not swaying the way he does sometimes when I hear him come in at night and run his hand along the wall in the hallway for support as he makes his way to bed, now he is steady, stands ramrod straight in that cold water as the cop looks at the license then passes it back and dad puts it in his wallet and they keep chatting though I can't hear everything clearly, something about a turn signal, the weather and the cop tells my dad to take care and turns toward his patrol car and dad waits, still in that puddle of water, doesn't budge as the cop opens his door and turns back with a grin on his face, nods toward the water and says, *that must be cold* and dad says, *it's freezing man* and I imagine his face light up as he laughs and finally he steps away from the puddle as the cop gets into his patrol car and pulls away. Dad puts his hands in the pockets of his beige windbreaker the way he always does and walks toward the house in his wet shoes. I close my window and listen for his key to turn in the side door, thinking this will become a story he'll tell many times, over many beers, in many bars, a story about one small victory in his life, not getting a ticket for whatever made that cop follow him home and he'll get a laugh from his drinking buddies. And he will break so many responsible father rules. Except the one about love, that will make me always ponder and attempt to understand the demons that haunt him and in the end, I will come to admire him for simply surviving.

Quick Wash

One bright afternoon in July a motorcycle hit mom as she crossed the street in front of the Quick Wash Laundromat at a strip mall on the corner of Jericho Turnpike and Elwood Road, when Teresa Simon was visiting from Kansas City and we were on the opposite side of the road at another strip mall reading movie star magazines and True Romance, imagining glamour in our thirteen-year-old heads; Anne Margaret and Natalie Wood on the covers with tiny waist lines and flawless skin, dreaming of magic days when impossible things would happen in our blue collar lives, then hearing somewhere in the background of our Hollywood fantasies the sound of sirens, at first in the distance then louder and closer until we put our magazines back on the rack and walked out the door past John's Bargain Store where mom told us to meet her and headed instead for the street to see flashing red lights atop emergency vehicles, almost dim in the haze of a humid Long Island summer, a gathering crowd of onlookers hungry for excitement, motorcycle turned on its side, no rider in sight, mom lying next to the double yellow lines, her eyes open, a look of pain and annoyance on her face, as if one more undeserved curse had befallen her life, but no blood in sight thank god and before I had a chance to breathe a sigh of relief, she said, *Y'all get the laundry out of the dryer* and I remember, in a bit of a daze running to the Quick Wash, stuffing the still-damp towels and sheets and underwear into a half-dry pillowcase, then putting it into the screaming ambulance, climbing in, speeding away to Huntington Hospital, seeing for the first time the sterile sadness of healing and death, the only bright spot the red Coke machine in the lobby and the doctor telling us she would be okay, and later finally getting hold of dad, the sound of his voice on the phone, the worried look in his eyes when he came to pick us up, knowing for the first time about the love in his tormented heart.

Lipstick 205

Most of the print on the bottom of the shimmery maroon tube with a thin gold band around the middle is too faded to read, except for *Wine and Roses 205* the letters barely legible, faint like a dream or memory just out of grasp, the rest hopelessly opaque, the lipstick itself no more than a tiny stub, but its scent lingers and reminds me of you and the way you always sat on the edge of your bed, near the window where the light was good and held a hand mirror as you applied the lipstick, outlining your lips, filling them in, pursing them to even out the color then smiling widely to make sure you didn't have any on your teeth and turning to me, knowing I had been watching you the whole time but never acknowledging my presence until you finished and I thought you were beautiful and always wished I'd grow up to look just like you.

QT Quick Tanning Lotion by Coppertone

Was my mom's triumph, her act of resistance
at Martin's department store, evening shift
fine men's clothing department.

No slacks allowed for women workers,
hose mandated. Silky smooth, flawless
beige, no black, deep brown or fishnets.

She said they suffocated her legs
an artificial layer of skin, an intrusion,
hot on humid summer days, expensive,

prone to unsightly rips like railroad
tracks running down her legs
marring the beige perfection.

QT was a miracle from the goddesses,
a weapon against unfairness and evil
disguised as femininity enhancers.

I watched her rub the chemical-laden lotion
into her skin, spread it evenly with no streaks
careful not to miss a spot.

The scent was distinctive like all suntan lotion,
reminding me of the beach, salt water
and crashing waves that pulled the sand

from under my feet and shot a thrill
through my body. But, the chemicals
overpowered like insect repellent

seeping into the soft skin of my mom's
tired legs as they turned a shade
desired to fool the male managers

who walked the aisles of Martin's
fine men's wear and policed the legs
of women workers.

Panty hose became a symbol to me
of all the shit thrown at women
trying to make a living.

Night Shift

In the photo she's on break
stands in a large kitchen
under the harsh glare
of a fluorescent ceiling light
stainless steel industrial sink
and countertop, white-tile walls.

She wears a nursing assistant uniform
dark hair tied back in a ponytail
holds a cup to her lips ready to sip
the black elixir that gets her through
the 4pm-midnight shift, V.A. Hospital
psychiatric ward. She smoked back then.
There would be cigarettes close by.

I study the photo for a long time.
Wonder what she's thinking,
if she's tired, worried about her girls
twelve and nine. They'll be asleep
when she gets home. It's a side view photo
a profile. I long for her to turn her head
look at the camera, look at me
and smile.

Midnight at a truck stop in Terre Haute, Indiana

parking lot packed with semis
all-night café lit in neon
country music on outdoor speaker
500 hundred miles that day
tried to make 800 to Kansas City
save the cost of another motel.
She said a truck stop
was the safest place to spend the night.
We called it our vacation
an eternity of highway promises
swimming pool at Howard Johnsons
air-conditioned rooms.
We knew it wasn't a vacation.
We were running.
Tammy Wynette's *Stand by your Man*
played as I drifted off to sleep in the back seat,
you'll have bad times and he'll have good times.
Hot humid air through the windows
mixed with mom's cigarette smoke
I was twelve years old.
Even back then that song annoyed me.

Girls, 1969

In a city park on cold swings we smoked
Marlboro lights and dreamed of boys
with mysterious hands in wild black
leather their bodies perfect we twisted
the swing chains and spun until dizzy
the nuns at St. James told us
our shoulders would become wings
if we went to heaven they would thrust
through our skin and we'd be angels
and the crisp communion wafer
on our tongues was the body
of Christ if we were good he would smile
on our insignificant lives send salves
to soothe our young passions
remind us of what to cherish and hold
when temptation flared and beauty burned
the clean snow melted into ugly pools
of slush and we may have believed
for a minute but we knew we'd never
be good enough for those boys
our breasts too small or too large
our thighs too thick or too skinny
and we watched the last leaves flutter
on winter earth streaks of red and orange
snaked through them like bleeding veins.

Seaweed—A Coming of Age Story

Before we were women, before blood and breasts and heartache, we stood on the shores of the Long Island Sound, skinny-legged girls on the cusp and gazed over the water imagining lands beyond the haze and distance as we waited for low tide, for the shimmering green seaweed to wash onto the sand, cover our feet like lace and we'd pick it up, string it loosely around our necks as if it were jewelry or a scarf of protection and security and we were transformed, our legs covered in powerful scales, wings only we could see and feel and we swam the dark depths of the unexplored ocean floor, through roaring seas, soared above ships and tankers and other vessels to far coasts of unknown cities and peoples who were both different and the same as ourselves and whose tongues spoke languages we had never heard before, but we could understand their words as if they were our own and they welcomed us and the women told us stories asking no questions because they knew our skin was too new to have answers and they shared their dreams, which we knew even in our adolescent hearts were on the side of heaven and told us of the stolen lands and names of the dead and the way tenderness and life had been seared out of those who came before them and how darkness remained, but they still believed in a new twilight even as death stars glimmered in the night sky and forests burned and harsh authorities were set upon people who suffered, heaped more trouble upon them and blood ran over the frontiers of new kingdoms and ancient homelands and though we were young, we understood at a level deep as the sea we had traversed and we listened to those strong and wise women until our seaweed began to dry and crumble, the green faded and all that was left was the women who stood before us, who had welcomed us as their own and they assured us we could find our way back and that we would have strength for a long time to come, though home would never be the same for us and we travelled back to where we had started and we rested on the shore, watched sea water lick at our feet, our legs now visible again, our scales fallen away and we gazed over that long estuary where salt water from the ocean mixes with fresh water from the rivers and we stayed on that shore until the tide came in.

Fountain Pen

A young girl notices the fountain pen laying on a Formica kitchen table next to a metal ashtray encrusted with old ashes, cigarette butts piled high, an open pack of low-tar Carletons a few inches away. Scraps of paper with numbers scrawled on them are scattered about the table. The dad is always calculating how he will pay bills connected to the little house no one loves. Cold rooms and slamming doors have carved invisible scars on each member of the failing family as fissures form in their American dream. The pen gleams like a jewel, its nib sharp as the tip of a knife—or a syringe for drawing blood. The girl wants the pen. It seems that it *should* be hers. It is not meant to scribble numbers on pieces of paper, total up the rent and utility bills, grocery bills, credit card bills, figure how much will be left from the dad's paycheck for beer and cigarettes. These things insult the very nature of the pen, what it is meant to be and do. She picks it up, presses the nib to her palm and watches the dark ink flow into her skin. She believes she has the right to take it. But, the dad will notice if it is gone. Even if he doesn't say anything to anyone, he will slur words to himself about it at the Formica table later that night or the next night after he comes home from Sam's bar and he will blame the close-to-breaking mom for the missing fountain pen and that will be a whole other thing to worry about. So, the young girl doesn't take it. She puts the cap back on and lays the pen next the ashtray. But, it is already ingrained on her psyche. The fountain pen is the thing she will need to

write past this moment
name the unnamable
explore the contours
confront the scars,

the hauntings
the hungers
the abyss of emotions
the words

all of which are a frozen sea inside her young body. The young girl doesn't know all of this as she walks away from the fountain pen on the Formica table. She just knows that it is beautiful and that she wants it very badly.

Who We Were

We were scrappy little girls
with skinny legs and too long bangs,
hanging in our eyes
on sultry Midwestern summer days
when heat hung heavy in our yard,
like steam in the bathroom
when we ran tub water too hot
and wrote our names across the mirror,
watched the letters slowly disappear.
Dense and vaporous,
the long afternoons we moved through
oblivious to the racing of time,
waiting for popsicles
and a day at the public pool.

We smiled at the camera
like we could one day conquer
mysteries beyond our imaginations,
make marks,
leave a trace of ourselves
across a clean slate of tomorrow.
Everything before us, we could be anything.
Enough time to linger
in our own impossibilities,
to make dreams out of nothing.

That's why we smiled so boldly
at the camera, no doubts in our hearts.
That's who we were back then.

American Night

I am the child who waited
in blue darkness and bare feet
for the sound of your car
keys in the door, footsteps
on linoleum, listened
for stumbles and steadiness.

I am the child whose heart
beat with unwritten poems
and scary stories, imagined
wonders and your salvation
puzzled the reasons
for such a lonely country.

I am the child who stole
cigarettes from the open packs
of Marlboro Extra Long 100s
you left on the kitchen table
with an empty coffee cup
and can of Bud Light.

I am the child who pondered
sadness and anger, remembered
your smile and stories of New York
its energy in your eyes, we raced
along its crowded sidewalks
to Nathan's Famous Hot Dogs.

Just a few more blocks little girl
you always said.

I am the child who waited
for draft cards to burn, flags
in flames, brothers to return whole.
Finally, I thought I understood
your anguish.

I am the child of spacious skies
and specious lies. Bury My Heart
Birmingham, Watts, Selma, Vietnam.
I am the child who believed anyway
in radiance, sunrises and cloud paintings.

I am the child who still looks
for you after all this time
in our dark American night.

II

Standing on the Long Island Expressway Overpass in Queens, New York

Headlights and taillights glitter
off wet asphalt like small sparks
of truth, I can almost see the old Chevy
the drift of smoke, stain on windows
taste the tobacco, smell the beer
on your breath.

The tip of my cigarette glows hot orange
as if I could write with its burn
on this night air dense with mist
and memory journeys through myself
the deserts and cities, dim streets
and midnight bars, all the drowning stars
and sunrises to arrive at this long moment
of smoldering time at once soft
and violent.

Motel 6

I sometimes pass the Motel 6
where you spent the last months
of your life, possessions loaded
in the back of your Chevy pickup
dreams scattered along yesterday's highways
loves gone flat like the last sip of beer
left standing too long
home a word you confused
with where you were going
never where you'd been.

That motel logo is a permanent marker
etched in my heart of your life
and death, a cheap neon beacon
of anger and sorrow I never understood
only feared would consume me
the way they did you, left you alone
in your own blood and urine
at the door of the Motel 6.

The Sound

Many years later you go back to the Long Island Sound, the word *sound* conjuring the splash of waves on the rocky, sandy shore of Crab Meadow Beach, that stretch of water between Connecticut and Long Island where he always brought you, where time now hovers, races and stops, yesterday and today separated by an invisible ether that silently calls you to the other side where nothing has changed and echoes are eternal. The voices of other beachgoers, squawks and squeals of seagulls, the tinny music from transistor radios. And the shrill scream of lifeguard whistles as they motioned him back when he swam so far out past the *no swimming* signs you thought he might swim all the way to Connecticut and the lifeguards eventually gave up, the whistles stopped and you smiled because your dad had won that small battle when you were beginning to sense he had lost so many others.

On this day of your return you walk along the beach to the jetty separating the beach from a shallow inlet. He liked to climb the boulders, held your hand to help you up. You would walk along the slippery tops trying to keep up with him. He'd look back and say, *be careful.* At the end is a ramada with a few tables. As you approach, you hear music. A man stands near one of the tables. He is playing Danny Boy on the bagpipes. There is no one else around, just this man and his bagpipes. And you. You stop and listen. Your dad's presence overwhelms. You feel him on this beach, this Sound he loved so much. You didn't go to his funeral. There were reasons. But reasons are like words. And sounds.

They trip you up, slip from your grasp. You can never completely trust them. He used to say, “You can do anything.” He never told you how. Never gave you much direction. But, his words stayed with you. Pulsed through your veins, your chest, your core. Sometimes, you still feel them. They’re like a hunger. And you still see him swimming out past the *no swimming* signs ignoring the lifeguard whistles.

Sedalia, Missouri

Through the window of the Bothwell Hotel
the sun sets gold above a white storefront
faded with age, this small city infused
with untouchable traces of the past.

You were so young, what did you want
back then? Did you tell him your dreams?
believe in beautiful eternal things
as a new life grew inside you?

I'm sorry I only half-listened when you told me
how you came here, the way children
do as if parents will always be alive
to repeat their stories.

I wish I could hear it again,
watch your eyes as you reminisce,
walk with you through Sedalia
where it all began.

But I can only breathe this humid
mid-western air that still holds
a piece of you.

Look at Us

for Mike

Look at us, you're eight
years old, I'm one.
You're holding me up,
looking at me
like I'm a miracle.

Look at us in the back seat,
a kitten in my lap
the color of rust.
You're smiling at me.

Look at us on a frozen lake
in a Manhattan park.
You look cold, you're hand
wrapped around mine.

Look at us, our family splintered,
broken, put back together, broken
again. Look at the dining room table
he turned over and you put upright.

Look at all your baseball caps,
lined up in my closet.
I wear the blue one the most,
always see your smile.
I gave some to the unhoused
at the encampment downtown,
I thought you would like that.

The Last Visit

The plane lands in Orlando and you take the last shuttle to Ocala. It's late afternoon. It will be dark when the van pulls into your mom's driveway in front of her mobile home she is so proud of because the place belongs to her, finally after so many years of temporary spaces, rundown rentals and reminders that where she stood was his, not hers. *Leave if you don't like it.* The sky is thick and cloudy, the air damp and heavy. You open the window long enough to take a deep breath, inhale the moisture that seems to hold particles of the past that have followed you for your entire life like a specter reminding you of long sweaty summers in Kansas City, running through playgrounds, wet bangs hanging in your eyes and the gloomy damp days on Long Island that you hated and loved and always wanted to leave but cherished when you were finally gone and held on to them like bits of your soul salvaged and reclaimed. This humid air is always the same even when it is different, another time, another city, even when so much has evaporated like parts of your life vanished, it always returns you to the moments, the days, the years when what is gone still lives. The airport shuttle turns onto your mom's street and you see the big oak tree towering in her yard. She stands outside the door under a porch light waiting for you, so small and frail, you could almost forget her strength, her independence, all that she has survived and when you hug her you feel every bone in her body. It never enters your consciousness that the world could continue without her. She will call you Annie as she always does and you will not be able to fathom how much you will miss hearing someone call you that, how much you will grieve the loss of her and that part of yourself called Annie that will no longer exist except in the memories that swim in the deep waters of your psyche reminding you of all the regrets and sorrows and love.

Cremains

Robert, the funeral home director
explains how the container disintegrates
and if by chance anything remains
like bones or metal pins
they will be crushed
the ashes uncontaminated.

He looks at our shattered faces
as if a grenade has exploded
debris falling around us.

The cremains will be pure, he says
and this word sounds like candy
a small dark chocolate mint
or those hard cinnamon drops
you always carried in your purse
when we were kids.

Robert's jowls sag
over the years the sorrow of others
has collected on his face
one death layered upon the others
in an exhausting accumulation of grief.
Maybe he feels our ache
for one more day, an hour, a minute
with you.

Reunion

We come back to this city of memory.
Dense humid air rests upon my skin
as if each particle of moisture
holds another dimension of time
and space, when chance still lingered,
we were too young to comprehend
impossibility and dysfunction,
and you held the fragile fabric of us
together, so tenuously together.

I hear the click of your high heels
against cracked sidewalks
on starless, late-shift nights,
the last bus home, you unafraid of darkness
and broken streets. Looking like a movie star
in that necklace with pale blue stones,
like chips of ice. You told me shadows
disappear when we keep moving.

I took the rosary beads
when we cleaned out your mobile home.
Seven pairs, I hung them on my wall
next to the necklace.

They shine a rainbow
when afternoon sun catches
and I think of your faith,
my profound lack.

But now you feel as close
as breathing and I dream
a bridge over your absence.

Revenant

On the anniversary of your death when absence has settled deep in my bones, you appear under the canopy of a velvet mesquite, a shard of moonlight falls on your shadow, the hum of freeway in the background, much younger than when I saw you last, brown hair pulled into the twist you wore when I was a kid, gypsy earrings dangling, lips painted red, hands folded resting near your waist and on your left ring finger, the gold band you kept in your jewelry box with the tiny ballerina that spun to the tune of Clair de Lune when you opened it, that box a whole world of sparkling awe, a story behind each necklace, bracelet, pair of earrings and you smile the way you did when we said goodbye at airports or train stations or when the taxi pulled away, a smile tinged with sadness and immense, unbounded love I could not fully appreciate until I had my own child and I move closer to touch you, feel the warmth of your skin, breathe the scent of your perfume, but you are gone and the wind picks up, a cloud moves across the sky and covers the splinter of moon, leaves me in darkness except for the dim porch light from my neighbor's patio and the shimmer of the ring beneath the mesquite.

Labor Day, 2020

In the hot tub with a couple of beers
my brother's email from Warsaw, Missouri.
Listening to Kris Kristofferson.
Phoenix burned, heat soared, I yearned
for time to race through our lives,
pandemic to end, separations to stop.
I longed for our dysfunctional family
together—anchored—silent love
taken for granted, absence unimagined.
I see myself turning
off Route AA onto Daisy Drive
down his driveway
where the sign says *Mike's Place,*
as though he will still be there.

III

Blood Sisters

for Jamie

I looked for you in liminal spaces
county islands a strip club
in the shadows of an interstate
wondering where you ended up
after the topless gig
in a dive bar on Jericho Turnpike
all those years ago
I imagine you smiling
in that subtle way sweat
glistening on your hairline
descending to your neck
and chest you were almost beautiful
in that place of stale desire
where we spoke of men
and love and philosophies
of nude dancing over the din
of jukebox music
and I finally realized
you would not follow me
to the desert land
you held out your wrist
and reached for mine
a glint of jagged glass
thin ribbons of blood on gravel
blood sisters you said

The phoenix bird

hovered over Black Canyon City
as we sailed down Interstate 17
in your old Chrysler, New Yorker
4-speed, gearshift on the floor
that immortal bird of resurrection
and renewal, larger than an eagle
crimson and gold as if on fire
its sound-song reverberated
through the car, over-powering
the Eagles, *Take it to the Limit*
playing on the stereo, the promise
of the new desert city a flame
lit by that bird born of story
soaring above us as we neared Phoenix
time eternal we could burn
and rise again, drift on belief
in rebirth, falling and regenerating
searching always for our own legend

La Loba

The girlwoman leaves home on a cigarette-filled night of last calls and all-night diners believing in symbols and stars, the Egyptian ankh of eternal life, the wisdom of wolves and intelligence of ravens, the chill of cold rain courses through her veins, no lines on her face, time not yet burning on her wrist and she travels the wet glistening turnpike of New Jersey, through mountain tunnels of Pennsylvania and all the open blowing fields ahead, rest stops and motels with cheap particleboard dressers and night stands until she reaches a searing desert city of sun and greed where Jesus walks the streets peddling promises to searching souls who stand in the shade of saguaros and can't remember who they are or how they have become strangers, their words colonized, made hollow and she discovers the factories and classrooms and men with well-shined shoes and choking neckties, salacious half-grins, Bluebeard's blood in their hearts and she is interrogated relentlessly as to who she is, why she has come, what she will do now and she does not know the many answers to these questions only that she must begin in the desert and the men in neckties demand her words which at the time seem a small price, they are only words and there are so many of them, but she dares not tell them, may not even realize herself, that she is searching for the wolf woman who stands by the highway in Black Canyon City or a Taco Bell in Buckeye, roams the backstreets of border towns, the empty trails across the Sonoran, the shimmering hallways and towers of the universities, the dry river beds and avenues of Phoenix and she encounters a woman in the underpass of a freeway, kneeling in prayer as trucks rumble overhead and another who lives in an old Honda Accord with expired license plates parked on the south side of Planet Fitness and one with tangerine-colored hair who walks along a service road in the early mornings and afternoon rush hours and other women in blazers with shoulder pads and briefcases who live outside their stories and the days and months and years begin to smolder until she finds herself in deep solitude, shattered from simply surviving and desperately holding on to wild instinct buried in her bones and she begins to put herself back together, salvages her lost words, unfiltered, uninterrupted and she looks into a mirror, her face now creased with journey and life and spirit and in the distance a monsoon wind lashes across the desert city, the scent of rain and creosote in the air, the howl of dogs sweeping through her neighborhood and from the reflective glass in front of her La Loba gazes back.

Damavand, 1977

The way the snow drifted
then raged into a blizzard
and the roadside café,
copper Samovar on the counter,
orange flames flickering
in wood-burning stove, walls
of tapestries with intricate designs,
a man behind the counter
in harem pants and dark blazer,
tea in clear glasses and Iranian brittle
with pistachios, almonds and cardamom.

The way the snow covered the earth
in layers of sparkle, buried the sins
and follies of humanity, created a sense
of significance, cohesion, harmony
and the words *home* and *belonging*
took on new meanings
as we sheltered from the storm
until it stopped and we continued
to the Alborz mountain range
where at the end of the day we stood
at the top of the highest ski trail
and waited for the slopes
around us to empty.

The way we gazed into the distance
at Mount Damavand, Persian symbol
of strength and resistance, 18,000 feet
above the ancient, troubled land

we had come to in search of ourselves
and it was just us and the pristine white
and the silence and peace and I imagined
that was what heaven might be like
if there were such a place
and an unnamable god waited for us.

Used Books

That afternoon I drove you to Bookman's, the backseat and trunk filled with all your books, you hoping to come away with enough to get you through another week; have the water turned back on, pay the rent, buy a six pack, some weed. Me, not fully understanding the depths to which you had fallen, how close to the precipice you stood. We hauled those mystery novels and history books, poetry collections, your huge nearly-impossible-to-pick-up Miriam-Webster Unabridged dictionary you kept laying open on your coffee table and all those Russian books from your college days into the used bookstore and stacked them on the trade counter. So many books I lost count how many trips we made, had to borrow a dolly to wheel in the dictionary and the clerk said to just leave it on the dolly, he'd come around and take a look and that it would be awhile before he got a chance to examine them all, decide if any were worth buying and for how much, so we browsed the store like we had done all those times before, always excited to find a treasure, a copy of a book we'd always meant to read or a favorite title owned at one time but loaned out and never returned, bookshelf incomplete without it, something vital missing even with all the other books because without a copy of that favorite book, the shelves seemed wanting and when we found that book we'd smile and say *Look what I found* and hold up Merwin's *A Mask for Janus,* Orwell's *Animal Farm* or Steinbeck's *Travels with Charlie* like it was better than pure gold and you loved books more than anyone I knew, so I appreciated how difficult it was for you to pack them all up and bring them down to Bookman's used bookstore and to ask me to drive you because your registration-expired, uninsured car sat in your driveway like a harbinger of things to come and we must have hung around for at least a couple of hours waiting for the clerk to decide on how much money you might get for your beloved books and when we went back to the counter, he told you he could take just four of the books, twenty dollars cash or thirty dollars in store credit and we borrowed their dolly again, stacked all the books except for the four and wheeled them back out to my car. It took several trips and you didn't say a word the whole time or on the way back to your house, the twenty-dollar bill crumpled in your hand, your fists clinched like a death grip.

Peralta

It is night when she returns to the mountains far from civilization's clutter, darkness broken only by the shape of light from a half-moon hanging over the ridgeline in that place of silent and foreboding beauty, stars like small sparks in the sky high above the desert floor and damaged earth. Jagged spikes of volcanic rock rise like hands in prayer from the canyon that slices through the Sonoran. They will meet at the edge devoid of boundary and unpassable borders where longing softens and fades in unbreachable distance. She will know when he arrives. He will have no shadow, simply a presence. The world will be a tale finally told and they will see the way it is made as the coyotes and bobcats, wolves and mountain lions do, feel its steady breath and know how to live amongst the destructions and devastations, the cruelties that have haunted all the circles of the sun. He will remind her of Raton Pass and the Sangre de Cristo Range, all the crooked roads and uncountable miles they travelled, so many loves now gone. *I always tried to find you.* His voice ragged. Sad. He will reach for her hand as they gaze at the broken splendor before them. They will leave behind fragments of their hearts that work into the hard soil. They will be a memory. And then nothing.

Watching Your Baby Sleep

You watch the rise and fall
of your baby's tiny chest
as she sleeps, the invisible power
of breath, thin thread of life
how easily it could sever.
Carlos Casteneda said, *You*
have little time left, and none
of it for crap.[1]

---

[1] *Carlos Casteneda quote is from* Tales of Power.

Interview with the Dean

His shoes are shiny and your breasts are full with milk whose weight you feel as you look at his ebony Oxfords not a spot of dust or scruff, they remind you of those old black Mary Jane Easter shoes polished to a sheen with Vaseline petroleum jelly, but not as bright as his, which almost blind as he asks you about your writing plans for the next six years, which will come quickly, he says, the tenure decision just around the corner though now it may seem far away it is something that must constantly be kept in mind, never lost sight of because every single thing you do from day one will be judged based upon projections of future successes, making a mark, bringing prestige to the institution and generally living up to, and your breasts have become so heavy as if about to burst and you are certain they must be leaking, but dare not look down to see, dare not take your eyes off of his which are glacial blue, because you do not want to seem distracted or intimidated though you do observe a slip of sock visible just above his right shoe, thin gray material, which looks like silk and matches his perfectly pressed slacks and you detect a flaw, a tear almost imperceptible, the only physical defect in this sterile room except the circles of breast milk you imagine staining your blouse and then he says something about more children, or another child, or child care, or children and careers, or women and children and before you can determine if this is a question this man who wears the slick shoes proceeds to say that you would be a target of opportunity hire, an effort at diversity, if, of course, the academy makes an offer and you note the stress he places on this conjunction, the power of the conditional clause and your eyes go again to the imperfect sock, the breast milk hot under your skin as if just boiled and tested on the inside of your wrist so it will not burn your baby girl's throat and again he says the word *"if,"* if you are chosen, you must promise them

your voice—
and all of your words—

Rocky Point, 1994

We watched fireworks from the beach
shoot over dark waters of the Sea of Cortez.
You were five, captivated
didn't take your eyes off
the colors bursting in the night sky.
Someday I want to ride one, you said
full of wonder and dreams and belief.
You will, I said. Every child
should get to ride a firecracker
as far as it takes them.

West Fork, 1996

You were so small
six years old, Memorial Day
hiking through the trees at West Fork
along orange-gold canyon walls
towering cliffs of sandstone
the shimmer of sun
through Douglas Firs
Big Tooth Maples and Aster
the gurgle of creek water
a day away from the city
you slipped in the canyon
your clothes soaked
looked like you might cry
I gave you my white shirt
it hung below your knees.
you smiled and scampered
along the trail like a little fairy
fleeting, ephemeral, my love
for you was boundless
I breathed this moment
into my heart to keep forever
to hold as a sanctuary

At the university

I create an imaginary budget
based on a Circle K salary
or Walmart or Amazon Warehouse
or the many barely-livable wage jobs
to convince and delude myself
I could make mortgage payments
on the house I should have waited
to purchase until after my fate
was decided by the ivory tower committee
but bought anyway partly as rebellion
but mostly for the child who dances
across my life like a fleeting wisp
of cloud story awing me
with her simple perfection
this wonder who knows
nothing of bad dreams
standing at the edge of a cliff
stranded in an endless ocean
exposed on a mountain summit
no way down, gazed upon by men
in ties, adjusting their balls
scrutinizing, I make the numbers
work on paper, fold it and set it on my desk
next to a small bottle with a rose bud
and pink glitter she made for me in daycare.

Girl Scouts, 2001

April has two tattoos left bicep
a rose and jagged armband,
once had breast implants
and showed the girls the silicone
after she had them removed.
April is my daughter's troop leader
who lobbies for gay rights
and immigration justice.
She practices Wicca,
has a pet python.
She is the reason
my daughter is in Girl Scouts.

The Photo

It’s a portrait photo black and white
taken in photography class
you’re thirteen almost fourteen
sun catches the gnarly bark
of an oak tree behind you
your eyes gaze slightly upward
to the right as if distance
might hold an answer
your face serious, contemplative
hoop earrings dangle
two sandalwood necklaces
your white t-shirt, grey hoodie
your cousin Brent died two days ago
your face no longer that of a child

All Grown Up

Nineteen ninety-five Honda Civic
113,000 miles on odometer
new timing belt, new water pump
new tires, Andrew Jackson Jihad
playing on a C.D.
as she backs out the driveway
heading to L.A. alone,
then San Francisco with Ida.
I think of the long hot desert
between Phoenix and L.A.
the traffic on Interstate 10
deserted rest stops
all the gallon water bottles
I put in her trunk
the AAA premier plan
will tow you any distance
how a house can feel so full
and then so empty
how it only takes one person
to bring the walls to life
fill the air with wonder
and love, faith in the future.

My mesquite tree

is a volunteer, growing in parched soil
from a stray seed maybe dormant
for years blown in on the wind
from a neighbor's yard or through the alley
in the kingdom of night as I slept dreaming
of wildflowers.

It looks forlorn as if uncertain
where it belongs, how it should grow
what it should be
appears more like a bush
than a commanding presence
like the wildflowers
blooming as if the world waited
for them, longed for their bold colors.

At times, I think the mesquite is dying,
skinny brown limbs, skeletal,
almost ugly. I could dig it up,
toss it for bulk garbage.
But, it came to me when nothing else
would and when heat flares
it becomes lush with canopy,
deeply green, almost graceful
and I am reminded
of the changing face of wonder.

Omar

A man walks toward my gate as I water sunflowers in my backyard that rise seven or eight feet from the ground, deep burnt orange-red the color of a blood moon, the first that have grown for a long time in this parched desert soil and feel to me like a sign from the earth that makes me smile when I look at them in the morning to see if more have bloomed and watch bees buzz from flower to flower covering themselves with pollen and the man wears a pleasant smile as he asks in a slightly-accented voice if I want to buy some tamales, $20 for a dozen and I open the gate as he tells me he has pork and chicken that his wife made and I say I'll take a dozen chicken, which he retrieves from his van and says *have a nice afternoon* and I say the same to him and for the rest of the day I think of his face and smile and the sound of his voice and they feel familiar as if I have known this man before and later as I'm eating one of the tamales I remember that ten years ago he was one of the workers who installed tile in my house and his name is Omar and a few weeks after the tile job he knocked on my door to see if I needed any other work done and I pointed to the rotted, warped wood of my front door which barely closed and said jokingly that the door was the only thing that needed work and he laughed but a week before Christmas he showed up again, told me he had a door in his truck from a home where he installed a new one and the old one was still in good condition and looked about the same size as mine and he just gave it to me and it was a perfect fit and I so wished I had remembered this and his name while he was in my driveway selling tamales and I thought of all the people who flit through our lives like fireflies who produce their own light and only live a couple of weeks before they die, these fleeting encounters often erased from our memory, but sometimes they remain with us and we cross paths again and it gave me comfort to know that Omar was still in the world, had survived the pandemic and gun violence and economic precarity and the menaces of our broken times and still had his smile and pleasant way of speaking and I hoped he would show up again with tamales or a door or whatever had come his way that he thought I might need, maybe just a smile and a hello that we both might need.

Where Did You Sleep Last Night, Lavigne?

Parked in the Planet Fitness lot
east side shaded in the afternoon
an old Honda Accord expired plates
windows covered with cloth
rear windshield cracked and patched
a million strips of duct tape zigzagged
across the glass.

One day I saw her and she smiled.
I asked her name and she asked mine.
Lavigne was a small woman, no longer young
she wore a colorful skirt and a wool cap
spoke with an accent, lived in her car.

Cervical cancer spread to her kidneys
she'd just finished chemo. She pulled off her cap
to show me her bald head. I brought water
in aluminum containers, she didn't like plastic,
a heating pad for her back, sore
from sleeping in the car.

She had a son but didn't get along with his partner.

She told me she was going home.
To Kampong Cham, Cambodia
seventy-eight miles from Phnom Penh.
She would be back in November
for more chemo if she was still alive.
She thanked me for being a friend.

I never saw her again.

I imagine Lavigne living
amongst lovely temples and pagodas
colorful French colonial buildings.
I imagine her buying fresh vegetables
in an open-air market.
I imagine her healthy.

And I think about friendship
its many shapes and durations
and how the world can shimmer
in unexpected places.

The Ghosts of Old Phoenix

Leave your house while it's still dark
just before sunrise take Van Buren
west to downtown, forget the freeways
they have no heart, feel the soft morning
hint of light, the way it whispers itself
into existence, rides on the silence
of time and the speed of solitude

pass the Blue Moon strip club
the cheap motels, sorrows and stains
you'll feel the ghosts, hidden dwellers
of fallen places and glimmering change
beneath the high-rise condos
and hip music venues they roam the ether
hold a piece of your heart

sometimes you find old fragments
of yourself along seedy stretches
of decay. *Why do you stay?* you ask them.
Because there is no place else to go,
the ghosts say. *And all our stories are here.*
And because of you.

Listening to the Grateful Dead as I Cook Christmas Dinner

I listen to the Grateful Dead on YouTube all afternoon as I prepare Christmas dinner, occasionally glancing at my iPad on the kitchen counter to catch a glimpse of the band, mostly Jerry Garcia in his black Fruit of the Loom pocket t-shirt, wild hair and beard, close to the mic, smile on his face as he sings, music in his eyes, an overall reverence emanating, reverence for what he is doing and I listen over and over, replay the video, transported from my kitchen and all the food I am preparing and as I sip from my glass of Pinot Noir, it all reminds me of you, back in the day when all we needed was the music, how we thought it would never die, how it moved you, swallowed you up, every note and chord ringing eternal, every lyric glowing unbroken and I remembered how you would take my hand when *Ripple* played and the dance carried us—

like water, like wind
how much I miss that part of you
how when you fell, you fell alone
how if I knew the way
I would have taken you home.

End of Year Love Song

For the fading blue, the long drift
of cloud white like sea foam
                                                  I imagined an ocean wave

For the canyon that opened to sacred silence
a single breath of empty space
                                                  I prayed would swallow me up

To the water that never fell
the desert that waited and mourned
                                                  the Saguaros who succumbed

To the raven in the winter Rockies
who walked right up to me
                                                  looked me in the eye

For JFK Airport on a humid summer night
the Van Wyke Expressway, the smell of the city
                                                  it felt like coming home

To the mighty Mississippi where I tossed your ashes
watched the current carry them away
                                                  you now a part of that beloved river

To the writers, the eternal groove of words
echoes of inscription that tremble our souls
                                                  and honor the fragments

The World We've Left Our Children

I am saying sorry
for the illusions
I wanted to give you
enchantment
Sea World dolphins
orcas, splashes of blue water
I am sorry for the cruelty
the ugly side of fascination.

I am saying sorry
for the poisons
we breathe
the bleached corals
the leopards and tigers
elephants and turtles
the species we endanger.

I am saying sorry
for the violence
the guns
the officer's knee
the never-ending list
of names
victims of the law
I am sorry for the boundless abuse.

I am saying sorry
for the slaughter
the wars

the genocides
the severed limbs of children
bodies beneath the rubble
the hunger and thirst
bombs and missiles
fighter jets
more bombs and missiles
and fighter jets.
I am sorry for the wreckage
the assaults on human decency.

I am saying sorry for the complicity
of "leaders"
in spaces of power
and on university campuses
I am saying sorry
for the lies
that fall from their lips.

I am saying sorry
over and over
faster and faster
I am saying I love you
I am saying I am proud
of where you stand.

The First Three Days

Day 1

I am stopped at a red light on a freeway frontage road, a silver SUV to my right. The driver's arm rests on the open window frame, his cigarette dangles as wisps of smoke curl into the air of this first day of a new year. A woman stands on the curb to my left holding a cardboard sign. She wears a wool cap, looks young, maybe in her twenties. Her skin is smooth, unlined, fresh. Pretty face. I catch her eyes and she walks over. I pass her a couple of dollars and she walks away, glancing at the SUV as we both hear the man with the cigarette yelling in a deep, powerful voice full of hate and anger. *Fuck you! Get a fucking job!* He drags on the cigarette, hits the steering wheel, screams those words over and over. We are the only vehicles on this road. For a second I hope an official vehicle of authority will appear out of the blue but, I realize it would likely be the young woman that would be confronted by the law, maybe cited, maybe fined and not the angry white man. When the light turns green, the SUV speeds through the intersection with an intensity that matches the hatred in his words.

Day 2

My daughter calls me from Brooklyn and tells me one of her students has been shot in front of the school where she teaches. At 8AM, the first day back after the holidays. He made it into the school before collapsing. She says there was blood all over the place. I think of her innocent child face, a time before she saw blood like that. Blood I never wanted her to see. I think of the 17-year-old boy who was shot. I think of the young woman the day before, the look on her face as the man screamed at her. I think of all the ways the world tries to break our children.

Day 3

In the morning, I make a fruit salad of organic blueberries, raspberries and strawberries for my friend's birthday brunch and gift wrap the little book I got for her, *How to Walk* by Thich Nhat Hanh, with soothing chapter titles like, Stopping and Finding Calm, Touching Peace, Taking Refuge, Walking Home. A swath of reddish-orange stretches across the sky. I don't know if I think it is beautiful or if it looks like the scattered glow of distant wildfires or smears of blood across a high school floor.

The Saguaros of Pass Mountain

All day they watch
beneath the scattered sweep
of rainless clouds, brushstrokes
across the desert sky
the cliff band along the ridgeline
glitters gold in the sun's light
as if in high testimony
to the resilience of these providers
of food and protection, no two alike
you wonder if they hear
the steady pop of gunfire
at the shooting range across the road
see the mansions climbing foothills
like advertisements for privilege
how many saguaros were sacrificed
for the sprawl, the border walls,
the apparatuses of security
the old hiker told you
they are spirits of wise ancestors
of native peoples, walk amongst them
he said, see how the saguaros stand
without question, even though
the world is breaking.

Scorpius

I have decided to direct my attention
for a while to the night sky
maybe for three or four years
or longer. Some of its magnificence
is marred by light pollution
but I can still imagine the awe
of auroras, meteor showers, galaxies
and clusters of stars, like Scorpius,
which is the most beautiful constellation
in the sky

and is Latin for scorpion
which makes me see in a new light
the scorpions who invade my living spaces.
I can view this nocturnal creature as a chain
of stars sparkling in the heavens,
so many light years from my life
I can't even fathom such distance,
but there it is, this cluster of 18 stars
a giant red one right at its heart.

And its immobilizing, venom-injecting
stinger becomes another wonder,
pointing to the very center
of our own galaxy. Imagine that!

I do try to imagine it when a scorpion
crawls along the popcorn ceiling
in my bedroom, as happened
a few weeks ago. I sprayed tons
of Terro scorpion-killer on it until
its legs and pincers stop twitching
and it fell to the floor.

But, as I watched it die I also
thought of the beautiful constellation
named for this arachnid
oblivious to the world of humans
and our madness, our carelessness
and violence. Unconcerned about us
except as threats to beautiful,
wondrous things like the night sky
and our own fragile existence.

To Carry On

Maybe read only the headlines
skim the stories, not everyday
a couple times a week, once a week
or listen to John Prine, *blow up your TV*
throw away your paper.[2]

Then, read some poems, lots of them
read them twice or three times
don't fret if the words hold mystery
let them be, give them space
words have their reasons, trust them.

Look at the night sky, the stars, galaxies.
Pleiades is made of more than 1000 stars
visible from almost every part of the globe
full with ancient myth and legend.
The moon, look at that.

---

[2] *John Prine's* blow up your TV, throw away your paper *is from* Spanish Pipedream.

Don’t forget the uncountable outrages
visited upon humanity by humanity
but make a list to hold in your heart
of some things you are grateful for,
that fill you with wonder.
Your list might be endless
like the stars.

About the Author

Roxanne Doty is a writer of poetry, fiction and nonfiction. She grew up in Huntington, New York; Kansas City, Missouri; and Nashville, Tennessee. She currently lives in Phoenix, Arizona.

She is the author of the novel *Out Stealing Water* (Regal House Publishing, 2022) and the poetry chapbook, *Hours of the Desert* (Kelsay Books, 2024). Her poems appear in various journals, including *Gyroscope Review, Amethyst Review, Cloudbank, Ocotillo Review, The Baltimore Review, New Verse News, The Orchards Poetry Journal, Lascaux Review, Third Wednesday,* and *San Pedro River Review.*

www.ingramcontent.com/pod-product-compliance
Lightning Source LLC
LaVergne TN
LVHW0906 5110826
845146LV00001B/405